EASY HANON

Simplified Exercises from Charles-Louis Hanon's *The Virtuoso Pianist*

ISBN 978-1-4803-3014-6

HAL•LEONARD® CORPORATION

7777 W. BLUEMOUND RD. P.O. BOX 13819 MILWAUKEE, WI 53213

In Australia Contact:
Hal Leonard Australia Pty. Ltd.
4 Lentara Court
Cheltenham, Victoria, 3192 Australia
Email: ausadmin@halleonard.com.au

Visit Hal Leonard Online at
www.halleonard.com

PREFACE

Since its first publication in 1873, Charles-Louis Hanon's *Le Pianiste Virtuose* ("The Virtuoso Pianist") has become an undisputed classic, practically the staple of technical study in music schools and conservatories worldwide. Departing on the premise that "if all the fingers of the hand were absolutely well trained, they would be ready to execute anything for the instrument, with the only question remaining that of the fingering [...]", Hanon offers a series of 60 exercises "necessary for the acquirement of agility, independence, strength and perfect evenness of the fingers, as well as suppleness of the wrists." The simple design of his exercises, based on easily retainable ascending and descending patterns, coupled with their reasonable length and progressive order, has contributed to their perpetuity: that, in spite of all the criticism that his work received by subsequent schools of thought.

The present edition presents a simplified version of the first part of the book (20 exercises), along with the major and minor scales, arpeggios, chromatic scales, repeated notes, as well as trill exercises. In an effort to adopt them to the level of the younger learner, the exercises were shortened and transcribed into eighth notes. In addition, the right and left hands have been placed two octaves apart to help the student maintain a more comfortable hand and arm position.

Following the exercises is a practice plan section (p. 24) to guide students to a deeper understanding of everything that has to happen in order to fully reap the benefits of each study; and, more importantly, to promote connection between the physical aspect and the broader musical design of the exercises. Hanon's ideal of evenness of the fingers, strength, and suppleness takes up a whole new meaning when viewed not as a mere physical by-product, but as a result of understanding how the fingers convey and articulate a musical shape in all its details: rhythm, accentuation, tempo, phrasing, and articulation. Ultimately, we come to understand that the musical intention is what primarily determines and strategizes the use of the appropriate physical means. The interplay between finger activity and arm participation can therefore vary depending on all the musical parameters.

CONTENTS

EASY HANON

Preparatory exercises to acquire agility, independence, strength,
and perfect evenness of the fingers, as well as suppleness of the wrists.

Stretch between the 4th and 5th fingers of the left hand while ascending, and the 5th and 4th of the right
hand while descending. Play each note with precision and very distinctly.

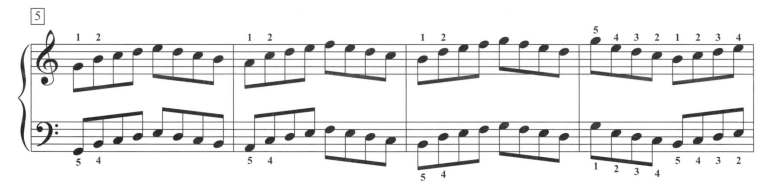

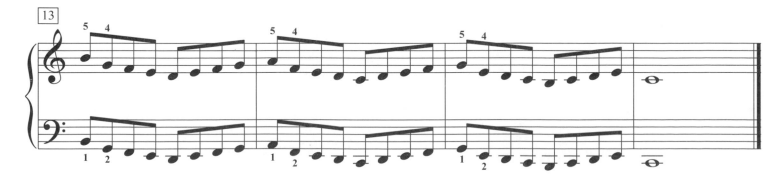

(3–4) When this exercise is learned, return to the previous one and play both exercises in a row. The numbers in the parenthesis at the heading of each exercise indicate the fingers that receive special emphasis.

3.

4

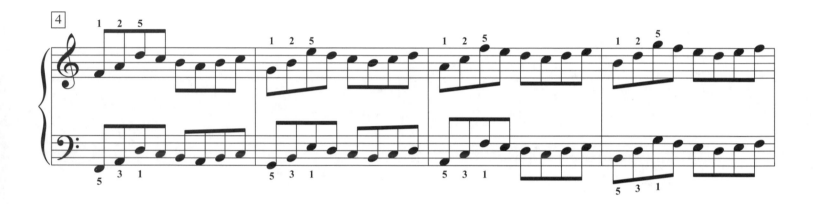

8

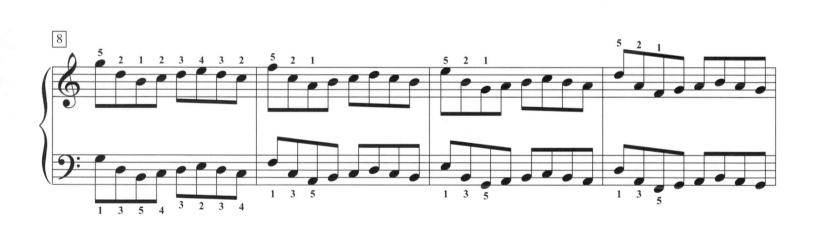

12

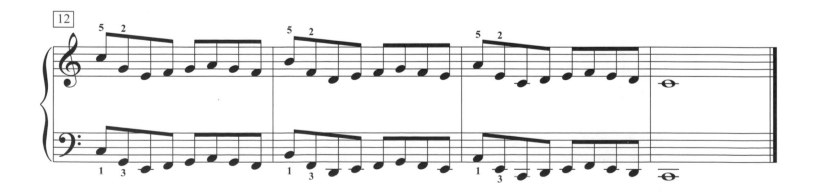

(3–4–5)

4.

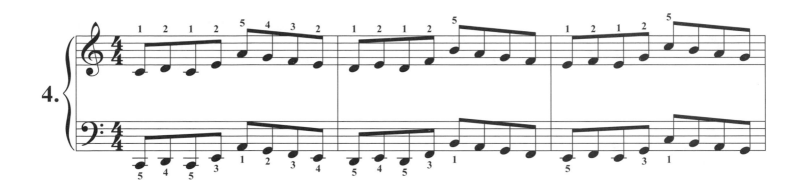

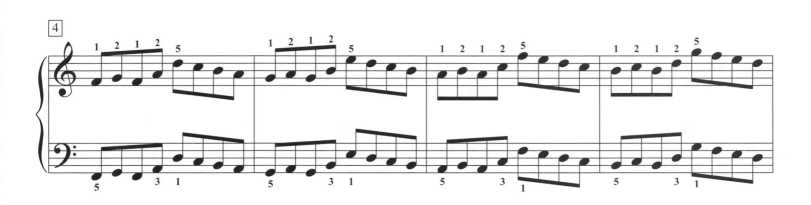

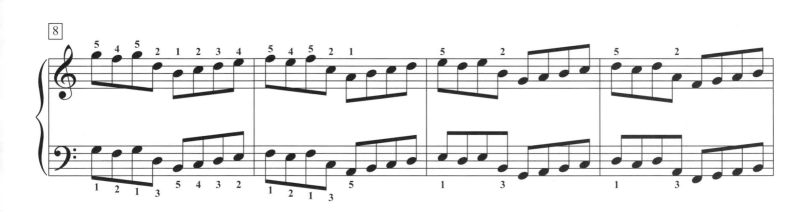

(1–2–3–4–5) Play with energetic and precise fingers.

5.

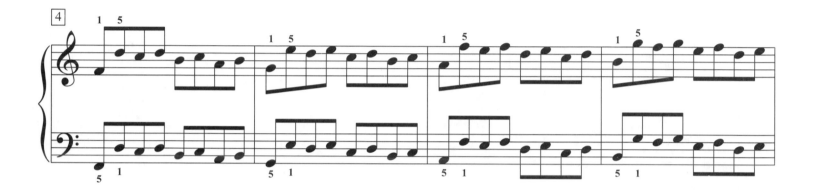

(5) Try repeating the already learned exercises daily.

6.

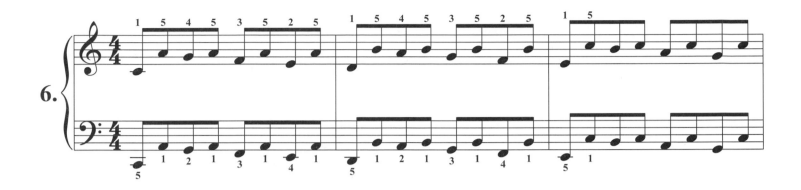

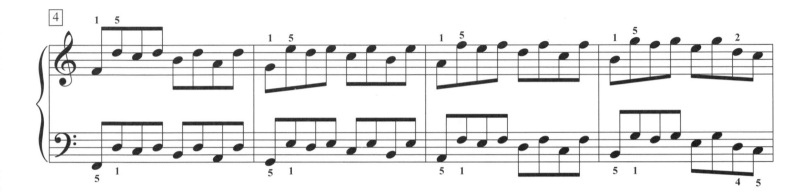

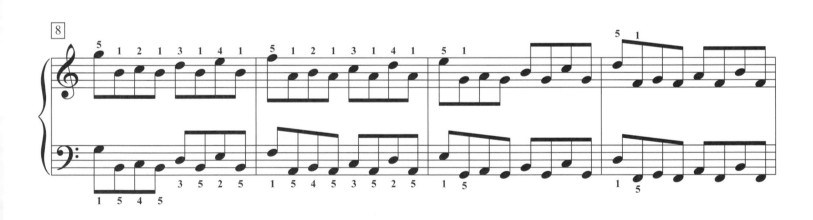

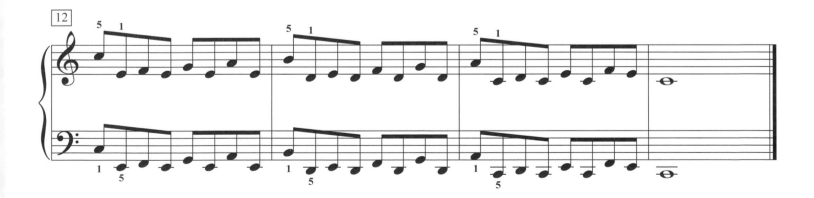

(3–4–5)

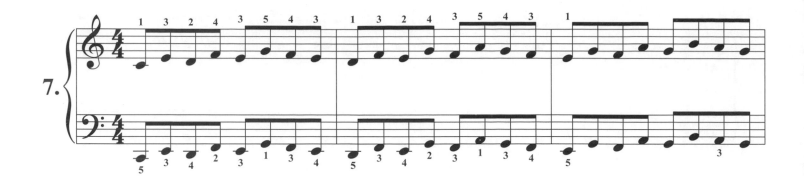

7.

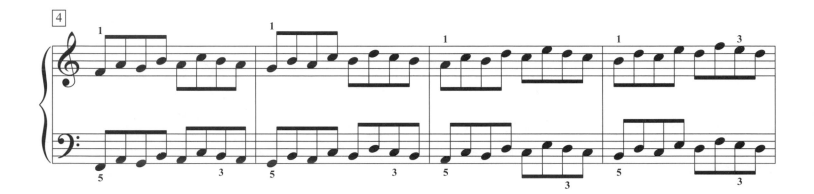

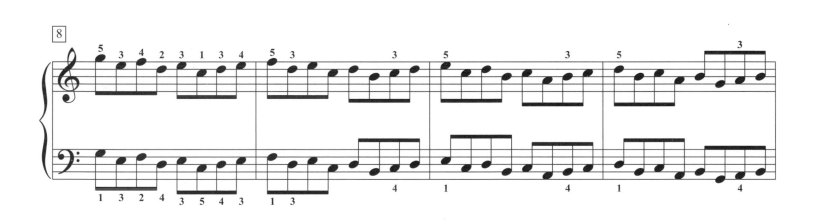

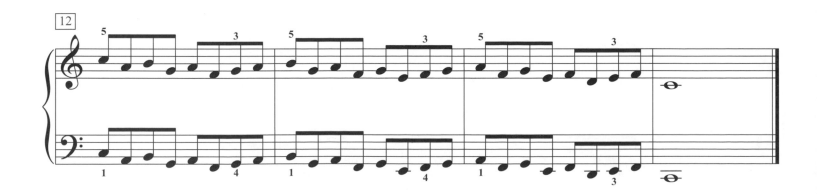

8.

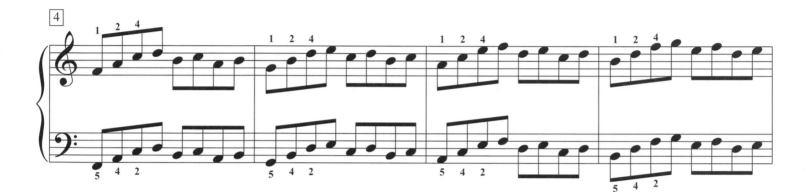

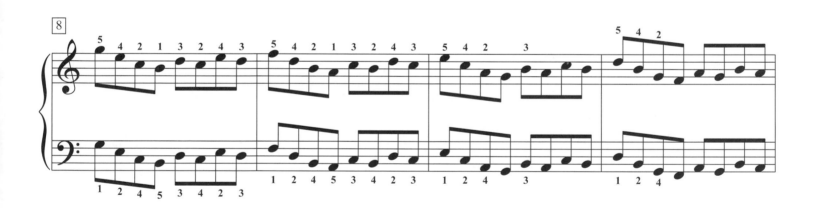

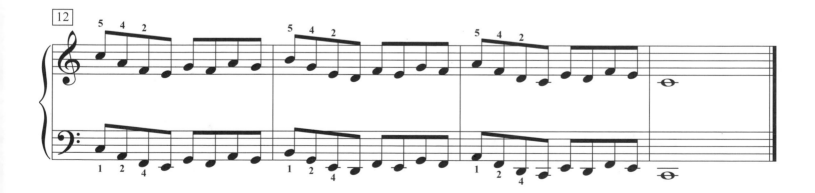

(1–2–3–4–5) Extension of the 4th and 5th fingers.

9.

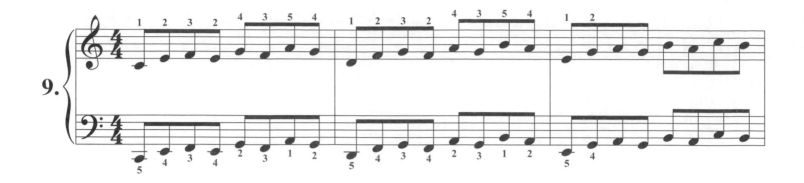

(3–4) Preparation for the trill between the 3rd and 4th fingers of the left hand in ascending, and the 4th and 3rd in descending.

10.

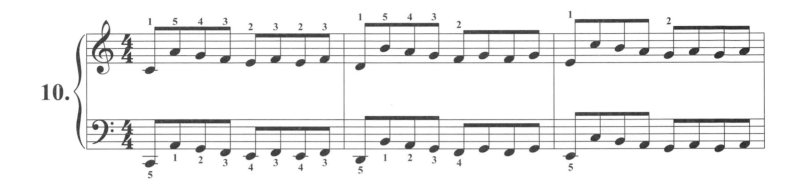

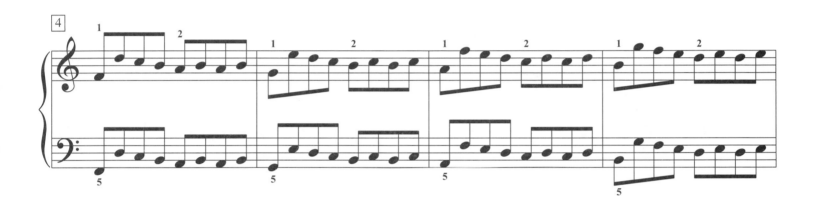

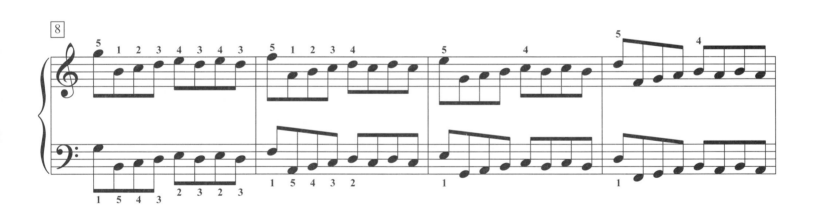

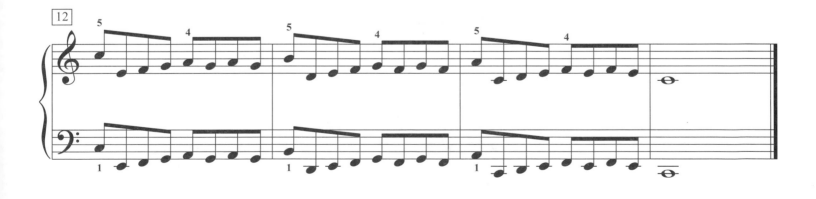

(3–4–5) Further preparation for the trill between the 4th and 5th fingers.

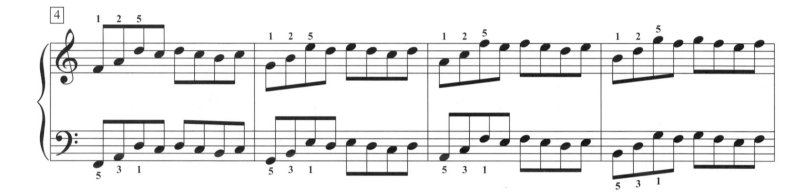

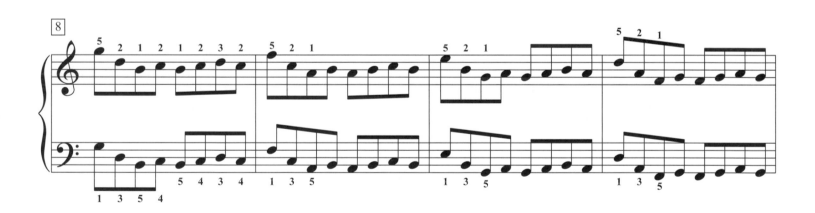

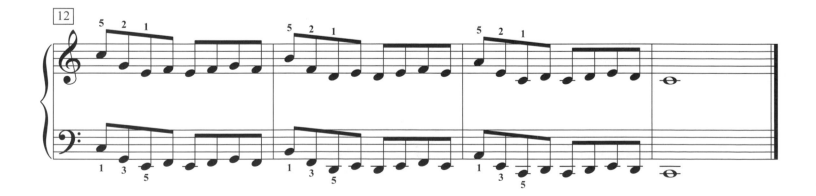

Extension of 1 and 5, and exercise for 3–4–5.

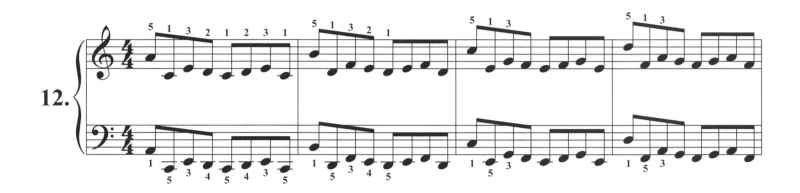

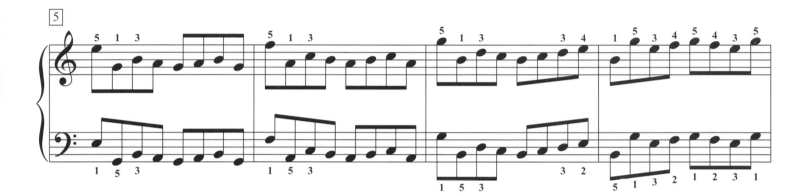

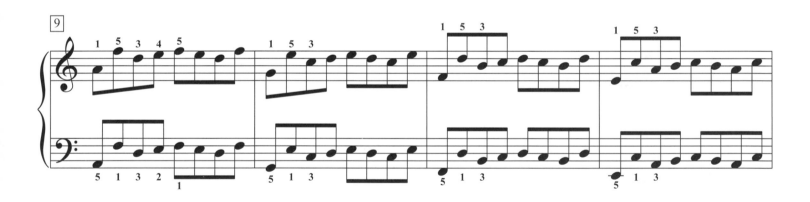

(3–4–5)

13.

(3–4) Another preparation for the trill, for the 3rd and 4th fingers.

14.

Extension of 1–2, and exercise for all five fingers.

Extension of 3–5, and exercise for 3–4–5.

16.

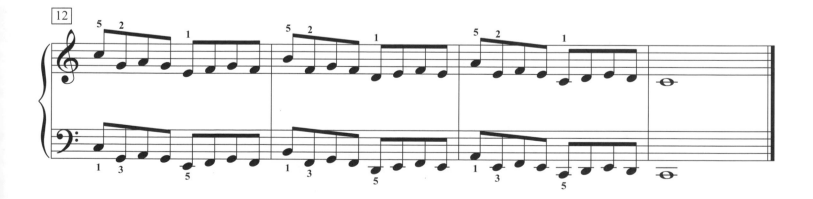

Extension of 1–2, 2–4, 4–5, and exercise for 3–4–5.

17.

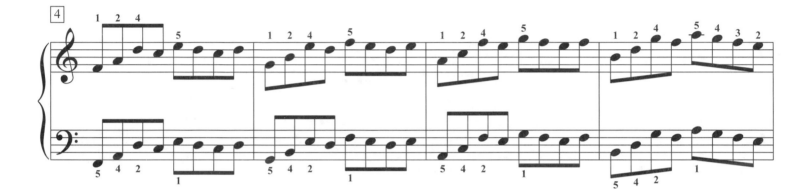

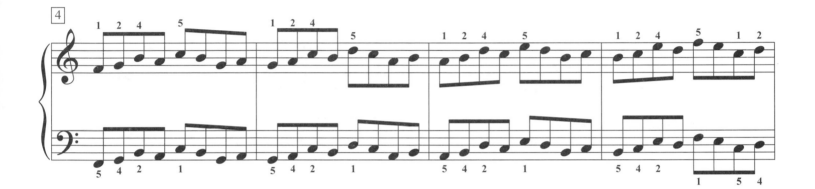

(1–2–3–4–5)

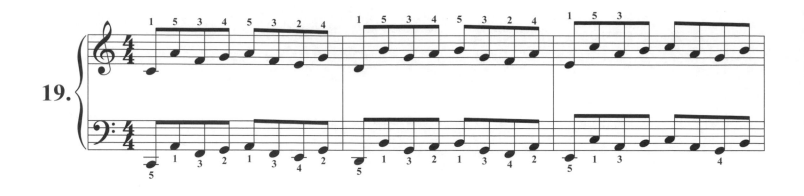

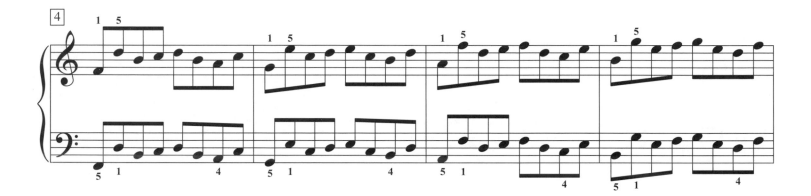

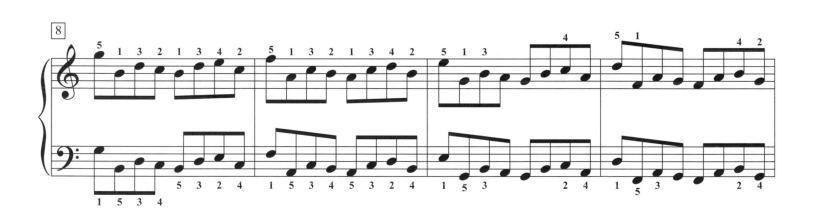

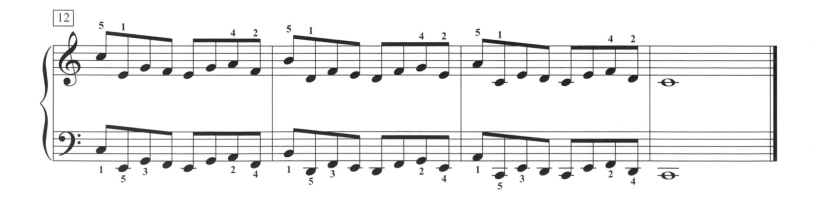

Extension of 2–4, 4–5, and exercise for 2–3–4.

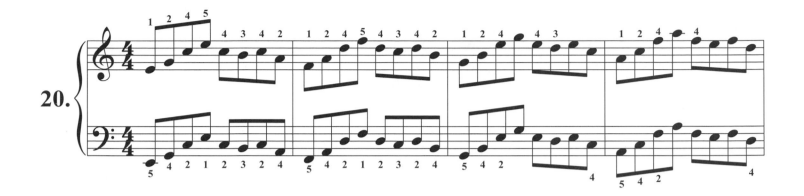

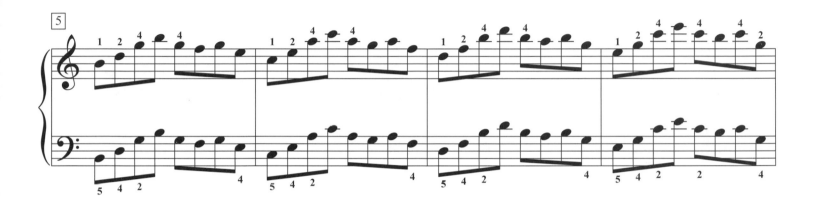

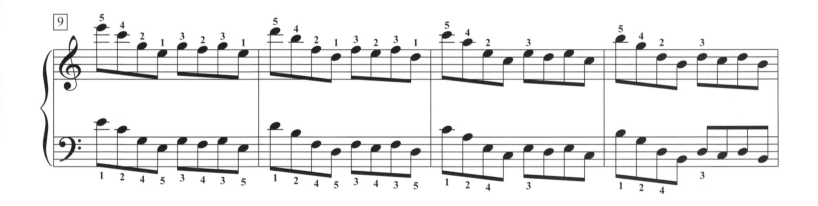

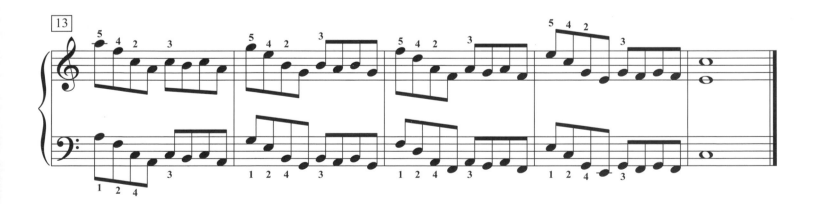

PRACTICE PLAN

Maintain a good posture while practicing the exercises, with a toned torso, energized core, flexible pelvis, and relaxed shoulders. The thumb should always be perpendicular to the keys and the remaining fingers curved. Shift the weight of the arm from the thumb to the hand side (fingers 2–5) and vice versa, using a smooth, supple arm motion, but without opening the elbow sideways. To this effect, the thumb is allowed to leave the key as soon as it plays. All levels (upper arm, forearm, hand) should form a straight line. Use firm and energetic finger work, remaining close to the keys.

The practice plan for exercises 1–20 is divided into four main categories:

Articulations   Altering the various degrees of long and short articulation aims at spurring the vitality and energy of the fingers. Depending on the type of articulation, the student is intuitively guided to find the right proportion of finger activity and arm motion in a natural and musically integrated way.

Rhythms   Varying the rhythm not only forms an effective way of promoting a stronger sense of pulse and a precise understanding of the rhythmic structure, but also helps with clarifying and analyzing the forearm motions. The intermittent rhythmic stops allow the student to feel the support of the arm on a specific finger before transferring the arm weight to the next one.

Transpositions   In addition to the energy of the finger, "finger strength" is a function of the proper alignment of arm and hand, which enables the transfer of the natural weight of the arm from finger to finger. To this end, constant flexible arm adjustments into new key positions, including ones that contain black keys, form the key to acquiring the kind of substance and evenness of tone envisioned by Hanon. Additionally, transposing fosters internal listening and an increased tonal awareness.

Doublings   This variation is provided only in a few exercises and is suitable for slightly more advanced learners. Reiterating certain intervals will reinforce distinct articulation of the notes and help with gentle stretching between the fingers.

All articulations, rhythms, transpositions, and doublings are interchangeable and can be easily transferred and applied to other exercises within the sequence. Equally, students should be encouraged to alter the tempo and dynamic both in playing the studies in their original form, and while using the variations. Altering and combining elements from all the proposed variations in an extemporaneous way is particularly beneficial, as it prompts students to constantly adjust their physical means to a new musical design using their own musical intuition and internal listening.

— Christos Tsitsaros

Exercise no. 1

Rhythm

Articulation (moderately, in a light but firm staccato)

Transposition (D major)

Exercise no. 2

Rhythm (feel a "scooping up" motion from the thumb to the rest of the fingers and back to the thumb)

Articulation

Transposition (G Major)

Exercise no. 3

Rhythm

Articulation
portato (slightly accented non-*legato*, flexibly but firmly)

Transposition (F Major)

Exercise no. 4

Rhythm

Articulation (heavy, firm staccato)

Transposition (A Major)

Exercise no. 5

Articulation (slightly accent the syncopation)

Rhythm (very lively and accented)

Transposition (E-flat Major)

Exercise no. 6

Articulation (feeling a strong swing back and forth between the 5th and the rest of the fingers)

Rhythm (play the sixteenth notes swiftly, almost as a broken chord)

Transposition (E Major)

Exercise no. 7

Articulation (staying close to the keys)

Rhythm (without rushing the triplets)

Transposition (D Major)

Exercise no. 8

Articulation (with an energetic fingertips)

Rhythm (rhythmic variations in exercises 7 and 8 can be used alternatively)

Transposition (A-flat Major)

Exercise no. 9

Articulation (with an imperceptible arm swing from the tied note to the staccato)

Rhythm (with a sense of phrase)

Transposition (F Major)

Exercise no. 10

Articulation (play this variation swiflty, in a light, yet firm staccato, exaggerating the accent)

Rhythm (evenly, with a firm but rounded and connected sound)

Transposition (B Major)

Exercise no. 11

Articulation (with a heavy accent at the onset of the slur, ending in light staccato)

Rhythm

Transposition (F-sharp Major)

Exercise no. 12

Articulation (the last four eighth notes in a heavy, accented staccato)

Rhythm (reaching the interval of seventh with a powerful arm shift, lifting the thumb off the key)

Transposition (D Major)

Exercise no. 13

Articulation (fingers 3-4-5 firm and supportive)

Rhythm (in a lively tempo, staying close to the keys with firm fingers)

Doublings

Transposition (A Major)

Exercise no. 14

Articulation (quickly, in a light staccato with firm fingers, keeping close to the keys)

Rhythm (insisting on a bigger accent on the fourth beat)

Transposition (D-flat Major)

Exercise no. 15

Articulation (try this first at a slower tempo, mezzo piano, and later faster, forte)

Rhythm (very evenly, legato)

Doublings (play this first moderato, mezzo forte, then faster, lighter and softly)

Exercise no. 16

Articulation (moderato, with firm, rounded fingers)

Rhythm (feel the arm shift back and forth between the thumb and the 5th finger during the sixteenth notes)

Transposition (F Major)

Exercise no. 17

Articulation (play this exercise moderato, with strong fingers, keeping the thumb perpendicular to the keys)

Rhythm (every note strong and supported, in the right alignment)

Transposition (E-flat Major)

Exercise no. 18

Articulation (rather quicky and evenly, staying close to the keys in all the staccatos)

Rhythm (Think of the first note of each four-note group as under a fermata
and play the rest of the notes quickly)

Transposition (D-flat Major)

Exercise no. 19

Articulation (moderately fast, with evenness and a sense of line)

Rhythm (moderately fast, with sound substance throughout)

Transposition (F Major)

Doublings

Exercise no. 20

Articulation (swiftly and vigorously, keeping the last eighth note of each measure
connected to the first of the next measure)

Rhythm (rather fast, in one sweeping arm gesture)

Transposition (B Major)

Doublings
a.

b.

EXERCISES FOR TURNING
THE THUMB UNDER

Thumb under 2

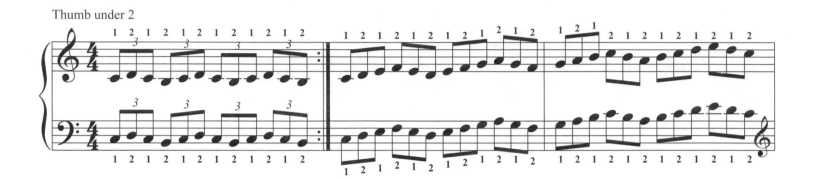

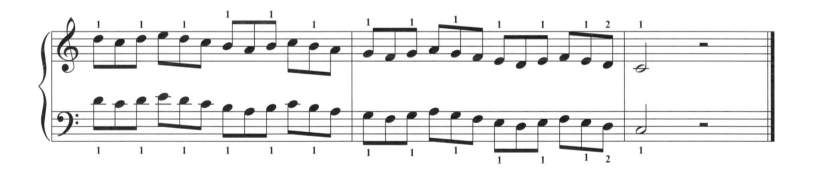

Thumb under 3

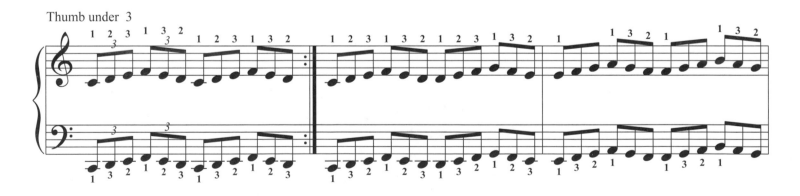

Thumb under 4

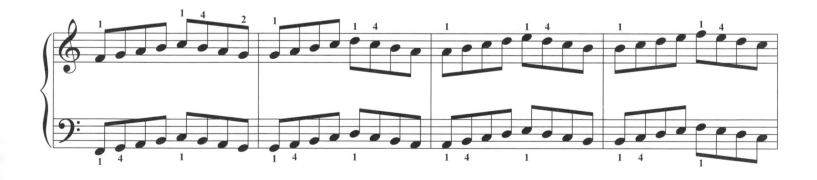

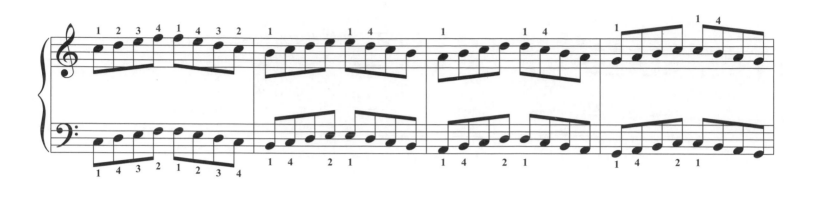

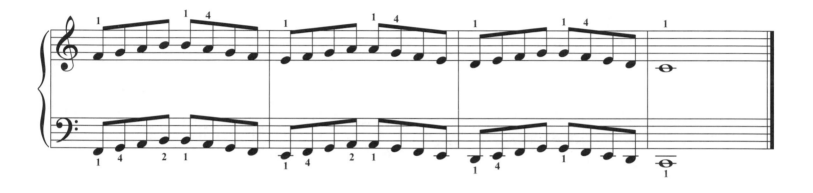

Additonal exercise for turning the thumb under.

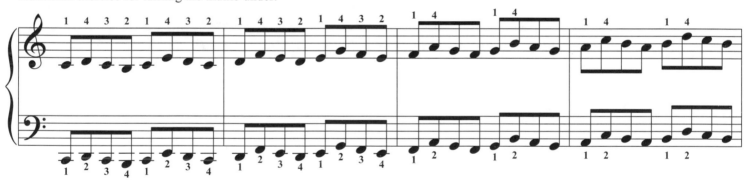

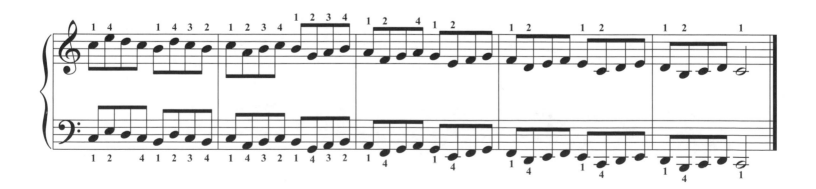

PREPARATORY EXERCISES
FOR THE SCALE

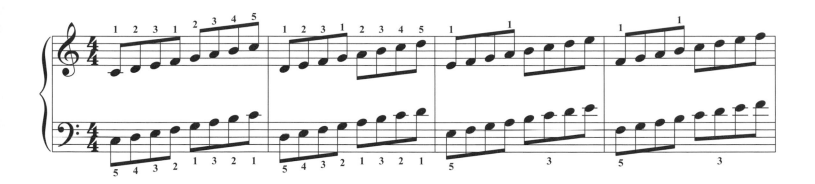

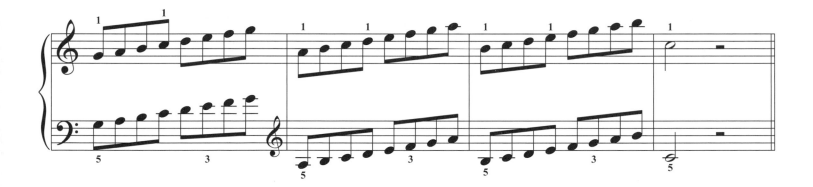

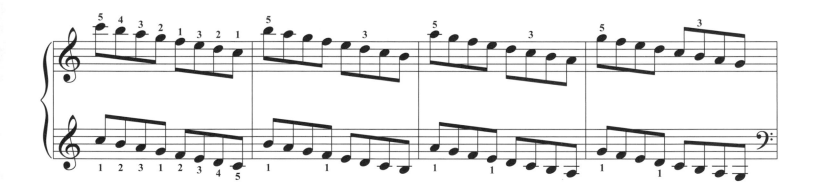

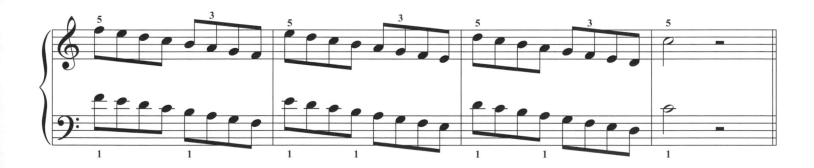

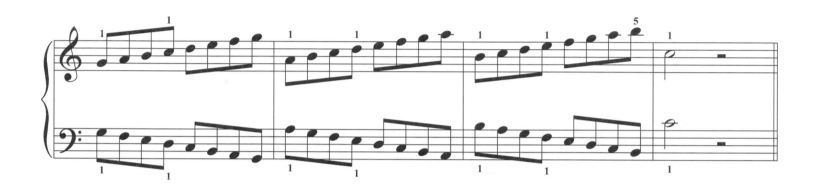

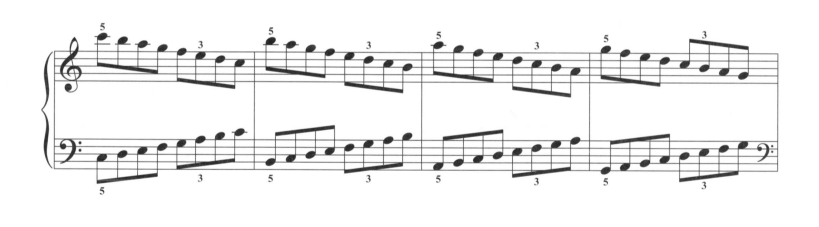

MAJOR AND MINOR SCALES

C major

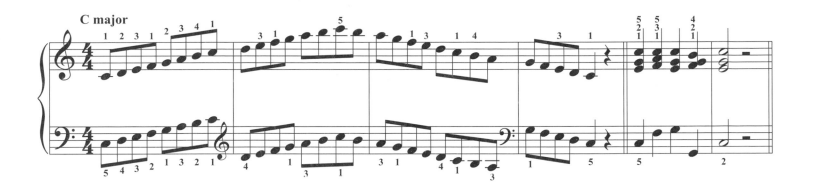

A minor (harmonic)

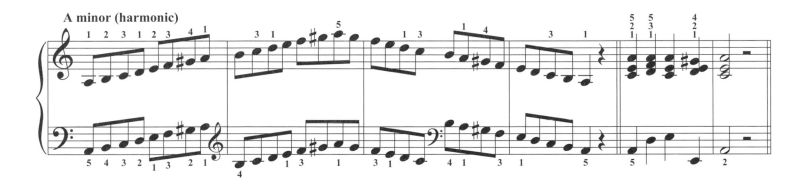

F major

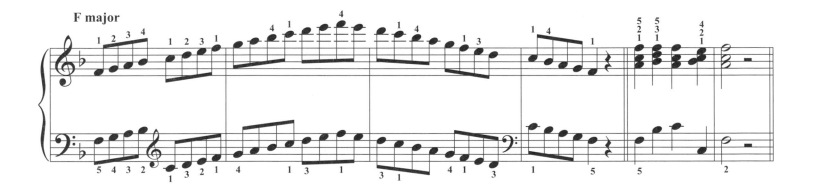

D minor (harmonic)

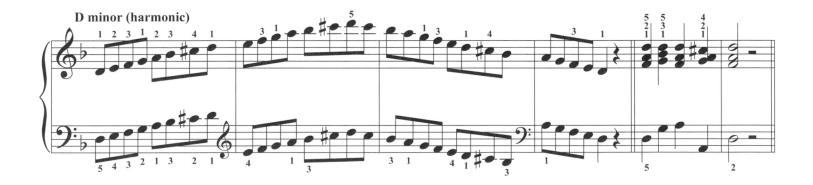

G major

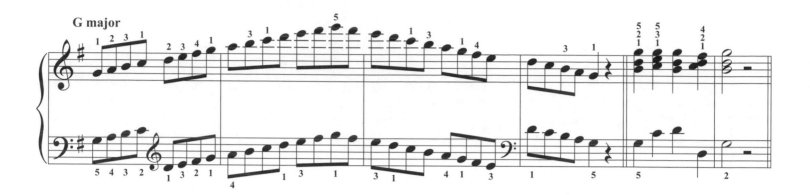

E minor (harmonic)

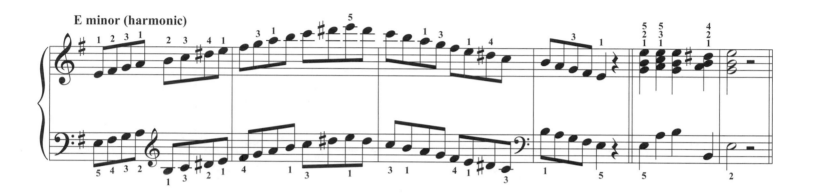

B♭ major

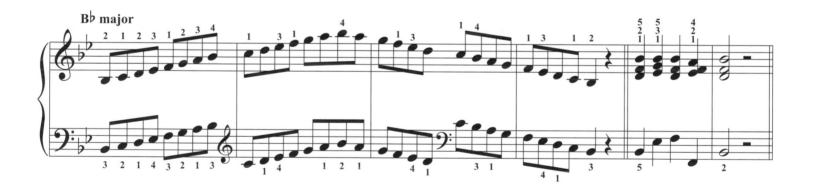

G minor (harmonic)

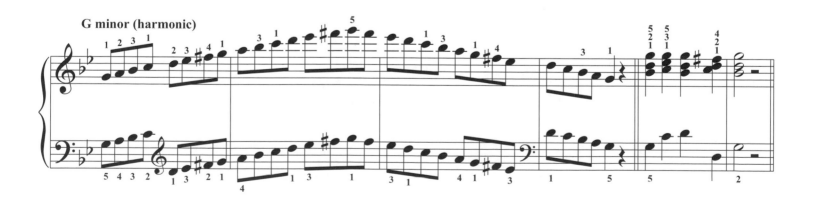

D major

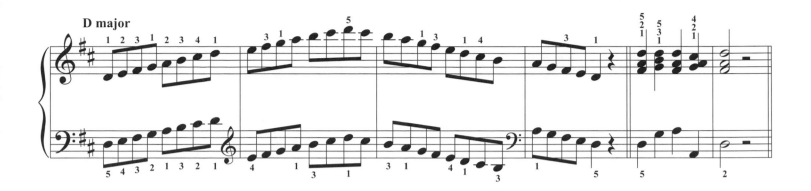

B minor (harmonic)

E♭ major

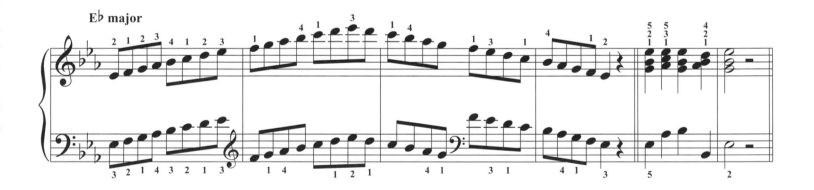

C minor (harmonic)

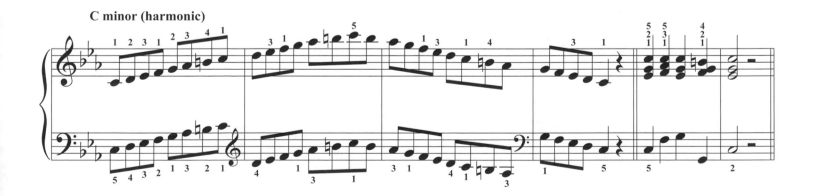

A major

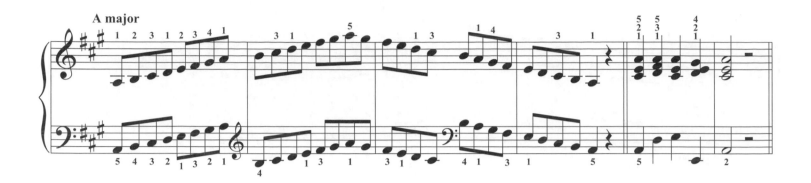

F# minor (harmonic)

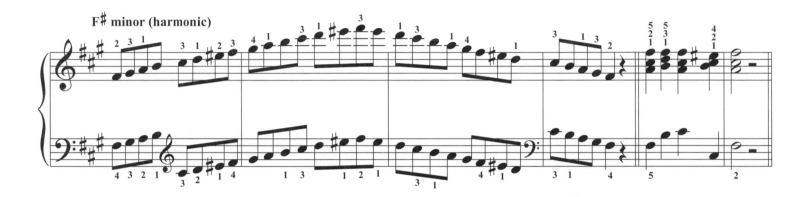

A♭ major

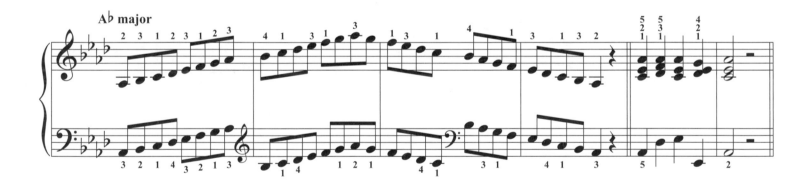

F minor (harmonic)

E major

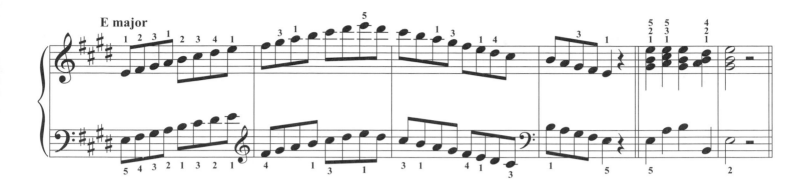

C♯ minor (harmonic)

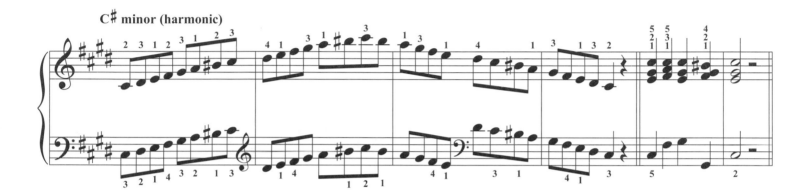

D♭ major

B♭ minor (harmonic)

B major

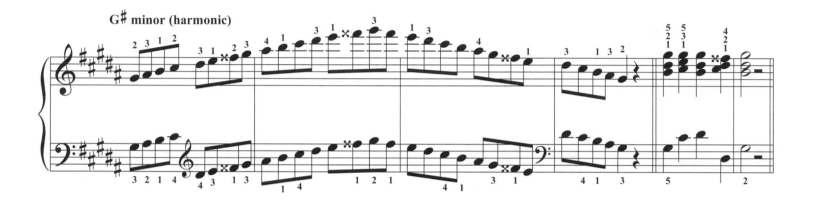

G# minor (harmonic)

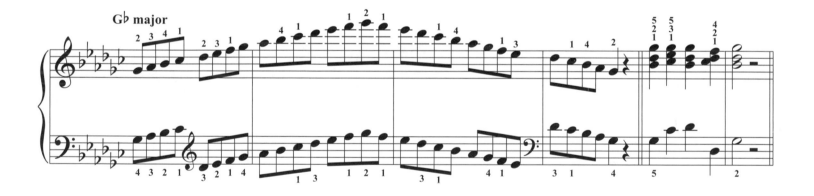

G♭ major

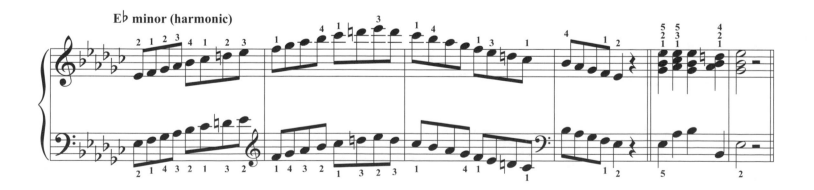

E♭ minor (harmonic)

CHROMATIC SCALES IN PARALLEL AND CONTRARY MOTION

1. Parallel motion at the distance of an octave.

2. Parallel motion at the distance of a minor third.

3. Parallel motion at the distance of a major sixth.

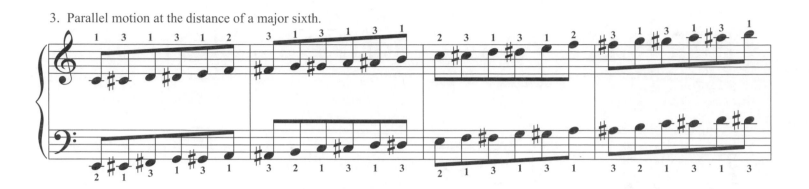

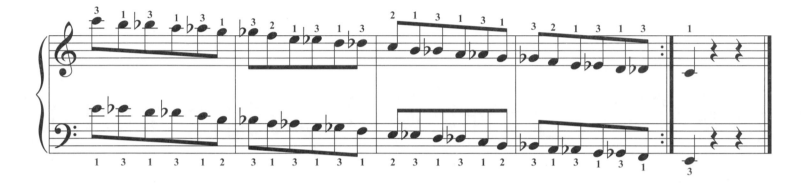

4. Contrary motion, beginning on a major third.

5. Contrary motion, beginning on the octave.

Another fingering recommended in legato passages.

ARPEGGIOS ON THE
12 MAJOR AND MINOR TRIADS

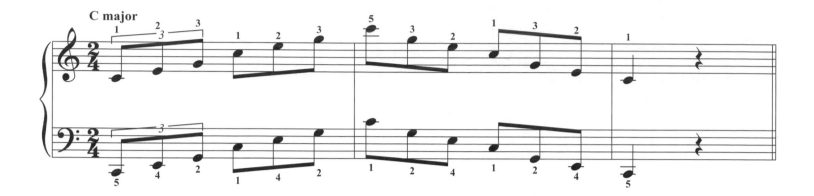

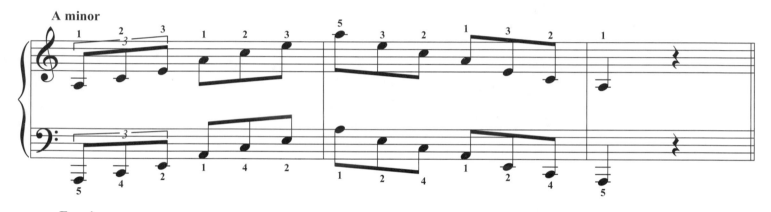

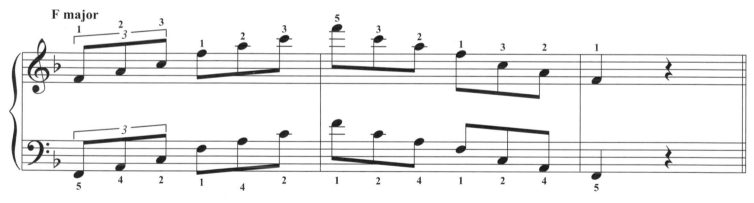

G major

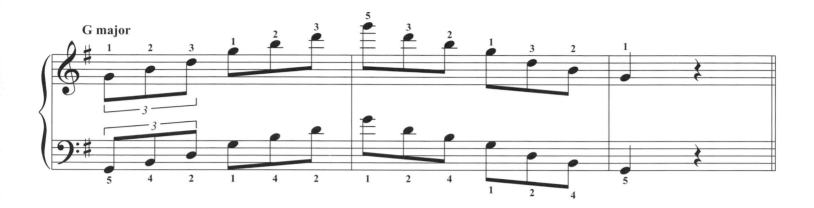

E minor

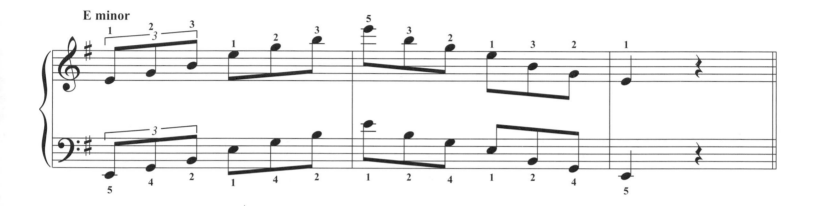

B♭ major

G minor

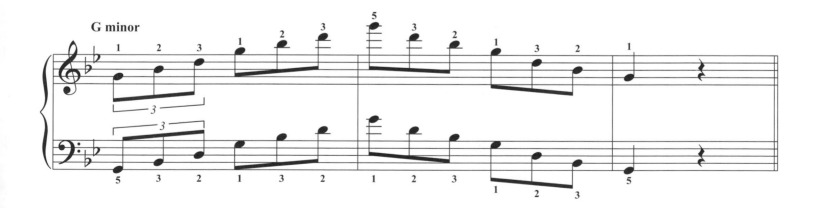

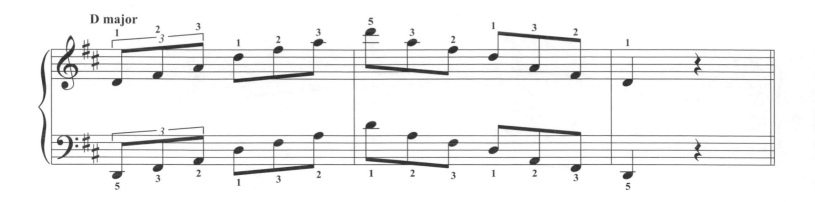

D major

B minor

E♭ major

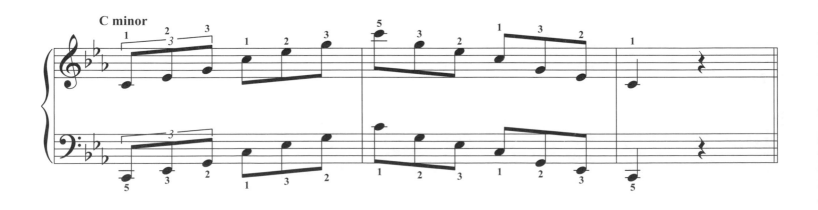

C minor

A major

F♯ minor

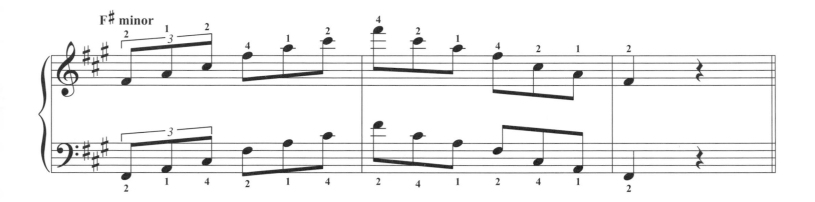

A♭ major

F minor

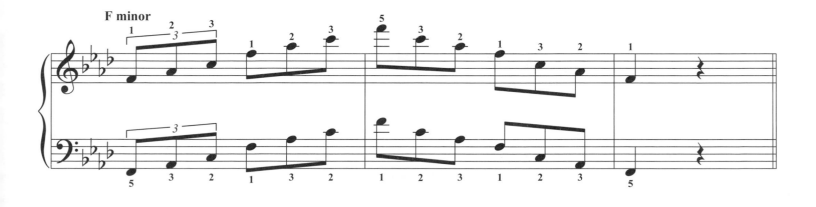

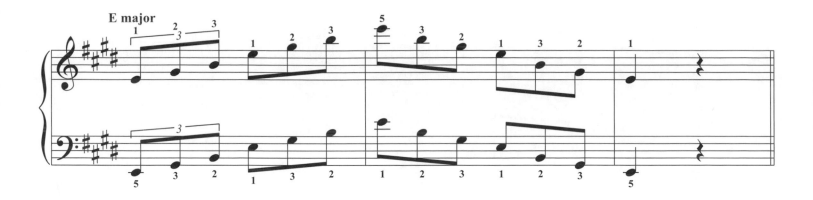

E major

C# minor

D♭ major

B♭ minor

B major

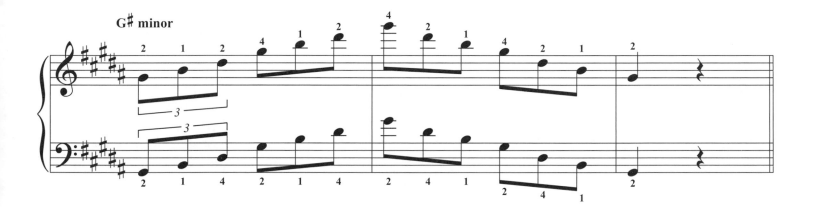

G# minor

G♭ major

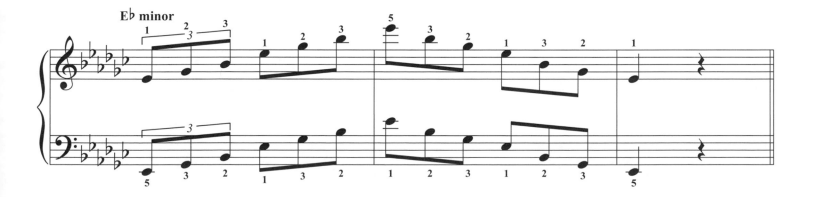

E♭ minor

THE TRILL FOR ALL FIVE FINGERS

First, divide this exercise into the shorter segments indicated by the double bars. Later, practice it uninterruptedly, making sure that the tempo evenness is maintained throughout. particularly in places where there is a fingering adjustment (such as in between measures 10–11).

Mozart's trill exercise

Thalberg's trill

REPEATED NOTES
IN GROUPS OF THREE

Maintain a flexible wrist, feeling a light swinging arm motion between fingers 1–3. In groups of three.

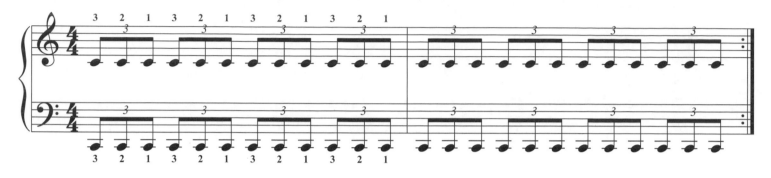

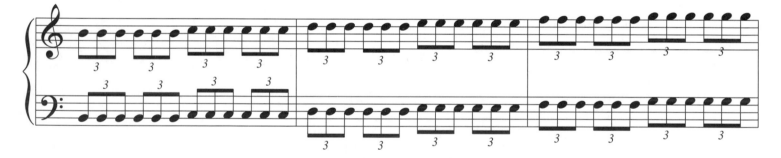

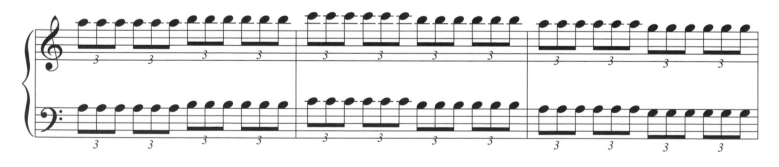

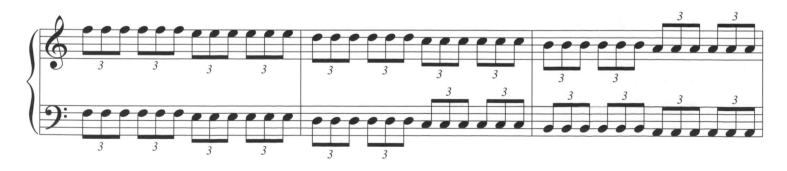

simile

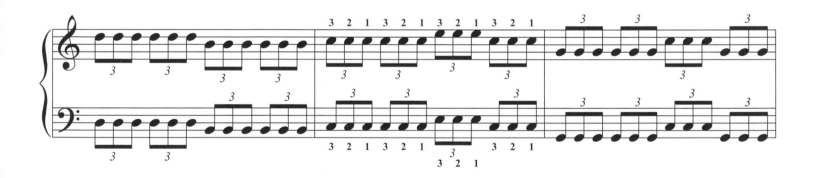

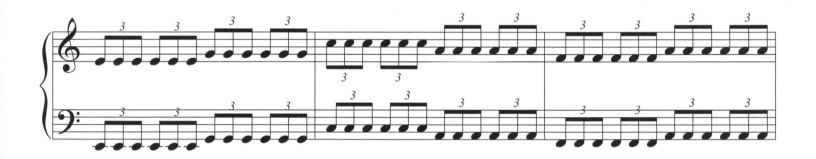

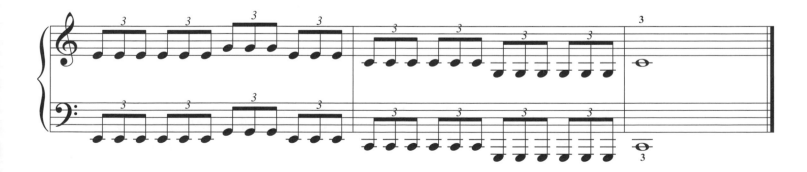